Detox Your Soul

A 30 Day Road Map to Loving Yourself

TAMI SHAIKH

ISBN: 1500779156
ISBN 13: 9781500779153
Library of Congress Control Number: 2014914323
CreateSpace Independent Publishing Platform
North Charleston, South Carolina

Dedicated to

My Parents:
Manzoor and Naheed Shaikh, with love and gratitude.

Table of Contents

Table of Contents

Introduction

First, congratulations for starting this journey! It will be full of ups and downs, tears and laughter, fear and freedom, and I know that that you will come out of it stronger. I'm not a psychiatrist or a psychologist, but I am a human being, a mother, an educator and a writer. Like many others before me, I have struggled with the big questions in life: Why was I created? Does God really care about me? Am I the culmination of my thoughts or do my thoughts create who I am? What is my soul's purpose? How can I find that purpose? These questions and many more like them constantly revolved in my mind. I decided to find the answers. However, I wanted to become a seeker, not someone "who knows it all." Departing on this inner journey has been one of the most profound things I've done in my life.

Anticipating the richness of my journey, I decided to write a book about what I discovered. Sure, there are many books already out there, including some that have helped me tremendously. But while quite a few say that we need to take care of our souls, no one really teaches us how to do that. We are told to meditate and find our way, but where is the road map for soul healing and eventually loving ourselves? How do we know which way to turn if there is a "mind block"? How do you rise from the ashes of despair into your own personal greatness?

So I decided to go on a journey to connect with my soul first and then to create a plan for others. Many people laughed at me and told me I was going through a midlife crisis. One of my friends even said, "Oh, so you think you're Oprah now?" When I got all that opposition, I realized that I was on the right path.

~

RECONNECTING TO THE SOUL

Here's the bottom line: sometimes we come to a point in our lives when we need to reconnect with ourselves. By ourselves, I mean *the real us* – not the one who has to have the brand new car every few years or the Gucci purse – but the one who resides in us and is like a magnet for love and acceptance. When I use the word "soul," I am referring to this real self.

I have always been a person who is driven by my spirituality. By spirituality, I mean that I felt a connection to God or what others might call the Universe. I also felt that there was more to God than the rituals that my religion taught me to do. As a child, I always had a conversation going on with God or maybe it was my inner self. By the way, I do feel these two are connected. God resides in our innermost being... our soul. The connection that we create between our physical being and our soul is basically by living in God's light. What is God's light? It is when we follow our mission, what we were created to do on Earth, which is when we live in God's light. As I believe that we fit together like pieces of a puzzle, we are all created to do something different and together we make the world beautiful.

For me, the time to reconnect with myself came a few years ago. Well, if I'm completely honest with myself the truth is that everything which has happened in my life was pointing me towards this connection. In fact, I have learned that making this soul connection is the purpose of our existence.

You see, we are born perfect as loving and compassionate beings... with a reflection of the Divine in us... and then life happens and we change. We become skeptical of the truth and light that lives within us and we lose our path. We question everything – our existence, our greatness and most of all our internal light. At this point, the need to reconnect to ourselves, by detoxing our soul, becomes essential.

MY JOURNEY

My personal soul detoxification started at a time when I felt like my life was going through a tornado. I felt like everything around me was just swirling at high speeds, and I was lost somewhere in between. I was running around like crazy during the day and not sleeping at night, trying to find the end of the tornado. Yet I couldn't get beyond feeling tired, drained and unhappy, and my health suffered.

My soul was like a tethered cloth that was sewn together with so many patches. The patches were then camouflaged with artificial smiles and unreal personal expectations.

When I started this soul detox journey, I was the biggest skeptic of them all. But I had no option; I had to go through it or I believe that I would have had a nervous breakdown. It was a journey of my physical body, which was trying to achieve a connection with the soul. It was a journey of saying good-bye to the old brain that had bouts of negativity and sadness and hello to a new mind that exuded light and positive energy. I actually had no clue exactly what I had in mind, but I wanted to give it my best anyway.

A SURPRISING DEVELOPMENT

Midway through my journey, something very interesting happened and I'll tell you about it momentarily. But first, let me admit, I had no clue who Arianna Huffington was! I had read numerous articles on *The Huffington Post* website, but was never curious enough to research where that name came from.

One fine Sunday morning, I sat with my coffee and turned on Oprah's *Super Soul Sunday*. On the screen, I saw a beautiful radiant woman talking to Oprah. Soon I learned that it was Arianna Huffington, and that she had a new book called *Thrive*. I so loved her story of overworking and trying so hard to live a successful life – it felt like it was mine. OK, maybe my life is not just like Arianna's life, but I was also a woman, someone who worked two jobs, a single mom, a writer, and a person who felt drained, emotionally exhausted, and kind of broken up from inside. I was at the verge of a breakdown. So I watched the show and I cried all the way through it. I felt like God or some kind of higher power was talking to me. He was telling me to stop and thrive, that I wasn't alone, and that my other sisters around the world – no matter who they were or where they came from – were silent sufferers like I was.

I was so inspired that I went on Arianna's website to buy her book and I found out about the California Women's Conference. The ticket was expensive, but I needed to feed my soul. If I bought the ticket that meant no Starbucks morning coffee for about two weeks and four extra hours of tutoring, but I just did it.

I went to the conference and it was the best thing I have EVER done for myself! There were so many inspiring speakers, like Jack Canfield, Lisa Nichols, Immaculee Ilibagiza, Sekou Andrews, Amanda Steinberg and (my reason for going there) Arianna Huffington.

I got my book signed and went home the happiest woman on earth. Arianna Huffington had given me her business card, so I decided to email her and tell her about my deepest desire – which was to write for the rest of my life, to touch people's hearts, and teach them what I had learned from all my years of pain and being disconnected. Writing always made me happy and gave me peace. So I wrote to Ms. Huffington, and she wrote back and told me that I could become an official blogger for *The Huffington Post!* That was when I knew that the Universe was coming to my rescue; it was trying to aid me in achieving my worldly goal. However, I knew I had to clear all the clutter in my soul in order to bring out my inner greatness.

WHAT I LEARNED FROM THIS JOURNEY

I must share that I realized something extremely important during my detox journey. It was very eye-opening and actually a bit scary. This was that in the past when I didn't achieve my desired goal, it actually had nothing to do with the outside world. It was my own brain restraining me from reaching greatness and achieving my purpose. It wasn't my boss, my jealous friend or my colleague; all along, it had been my own inner insecurities. I would have defeating thoughts pollute my mind and reduce my self-esteem. One of these thoughts was that if I didn't achieve my goal on my first try, people would laugh at me and I would feel humiliated. However, I have come to believe that when people humiliate you, it's only because you allow yourself to believe what they are saying. A friend of mine once said to me, "Tami, they can't humiliate you unless you give people permission to do that."

If we don't get a job we wanted, the promotion we're looking for, or that desired opportunity, it's no one else's fault. The fault lies deep within our soul. We don't get the opportunity because we don't believe in ourselves enough or we fear the unknown. I truly believe that if we can conquer our own fears, we can achieve any goal we want. So in order to achieve greatness at work or in a certain relationship, we need to meet our superior self and get rid of our inferior insecurities. If we can open our hearts to the truth of our own greatness, we can spill that energy of greatness outside into the world.

KEEP ON PUSHING THROUGH

*S*tarting this journey was hard, I won't lie to you. I had lived a certain way for over 40 years and now I was going to change that. I took the first 30 days to do my research. What needed to be done? Where would I get the info? I decided to go to the experts. I read many books including *Thrive* by Arianna Huffington, *Instinct* by T.D. Jakes and *The Success Principles* by Jack Canfield. I read about Mother Teresa, Nelson Mandela and so many others who had made a positive impact on the world. Another thing is that I kept watching Oprah's *Super Soul Sunday,* which I think had a huge impact on me.

When I was emotionally ready, I decided to jump right in and start doing the exercises and actions I had put together. I took some time every morning to do one of them, and the main theme would become my mantra for the day. The next day, I would incorporate something new, while keeping the previous ideas in mind.

Admittedly, this takes some work. You'll be facing things that you have been avoiding for years. For instance, when I started the journey, I decided to spend more time doing things that I enjoyed. But it was so hard; I felt anxiety and panic every time I tried. My soul just wasn't used to me feeding it, so it went all crazy on me. These things will happen, but continue to push you. The fact that you are able to face your real self will eventually give you more peace and serenity.

JUMPING IN

*I*f you want to go through this detox, I suggest that you wake up 10 minutes earlier and go to bed 10 minutes later. Those are the times when you are closest to your superior soul. In other words, that's when you're one with the Universe. During the day, we have the chatter of everyday life. You can't detox your soul, if you're not fully aligned with your mind, body and soul.

You will start Day 1 with reading from the book and throughout the day you will incorporate the strategies into your daily life. Before you go to sleep, you will then open "Notes" section after Day 1 and write about your day, the exercises, and what you have achieved that day. You will do this every day until Day 30.

Are you ready? Here's to celebrating our soul and the beauty that lies within!!

Day 1

Begin to Tap into Your Goal

*T*his detox might not work for you if you have goals like "I will win the lottery" or "I will be a millionaire in a month." This is a journey of the soul... of the spirit. If you're not willing to laugh, cry and just jump right into your authentic self, then please stop now.

Your ultimate goal should be something in your soul that you really want or it could be something that you want to get rid of or that is pulling you down. It could even be something that you're amazing at but you've hidden it from the world, and now you want to bring it out. What were you created to do? What is it that makes your heart smile? This is a goal that will enhance your life or make you feel better from the inside out. Feeling good from the inside will exude a level of positivity and confidence that will definitely improve your life.

I think one of the biggest mistakes we make is that we know everyone around us – what gift a friend would want for their birthday, what our kids like, what a partner needs – but how many of us know what it is that we want? So in order to achieve what your soul is longing for, you first need to know what it is. Dig deep! Start by writing down five things that you feel you could change about yourself, and one ultimate goal of what you want to achieve. For me, it was to be more forgiving, to bring more positive people into my life, to not stress about the small things, to notice the beauty around me, and to listen to my heart. What

I wanted was to write and tell the stories that lived in me. Those were my goals.

The truth is that in order to find outward peace we need to have calmness within. So if you want to achieve success, with a sense of joy and passion, make sure your soul has reached a place where it is at peace with itself. I say that because I feel that the chaos in the world is a metaphor for the chaos that resides inside our souls.

Go ahead think of five improvements and enhancements in your soul that you could make. Like I said, change from within = change in the outside world. Then also think about how making those changes could allow you to reach your Ultimate Goal. It's OK if you're not completely clear right now about what your Ultimate Goal is. We'll work more on that, but let it start to come forward. Today you will mainly get to know your five smaller goals and spend the whole day just thinking about how you could achieve these goals and incorporate them into your life. By finding your goals and striving to achieve them, you eventually rid your soul of the toxins that linger inside. As now you are working for a bigger purpose which is a healthy soul.

At this point, I want to share an experience I had with you. A student of mine, who was seven years old, always said that she wanted to be an artist – "a drawer" in her words. Yet when she would sit down to draw, she couldn't draw a straight line using a ruler. When she would have to draw something specific, she just couldn't. However, whenever she was able to just draw freely, it was the most beautiful thing I had ever seen. She would put different shapes together and create some abstract art type of drawing, which was beautiful, interesting and intriguing. This little girl of seven didn't want to be told what to draw; she was an artist, a "drawer" in her own mind. So learn from her today, and let whatever Ultimate Goal that your heart desires begin to speak to you.

NOTES

_____

_____

_____

_____

_____

_____

_____

_____

_____

_____

_____

_____

_____

_____

_____

NOTES

_____

_____

_____

_____

_____

_____

_____

_____

_____

_____

_____

_____

_____

_____

Day 2

Start with the End in Mind

The first day that I decided to start this life-changing journey, I was scared and nervous. As I woke up that morning, my preconditioned mind started to tell me that this was all really dumb, and I didn't need a soul detox. The chatter in my brain just went on and on. I think as humans, we are so scared of the unknown that we just rip ourselves apart. We know we are destined for greatness, yet we aren't ready to fight the Battle of the Logical Mind and the Superior Soul. So please, if you want to quit during these 30 days, just don't. You are far superior to what your brain tells you. Hey, it is only using 20% of its own self!!!!

The first thing to do for this daily work is to find your perfect space. It doesn't have to be the same space every day. One day you could just feel like sitting on your bed, other days taking a seat at your desk, and on some days even placing yourself out in the yard or in a park on the grass. But ask yourself, "Where do I want to be today? Where will I be at peace?" Once you have figured that out, take this book and read what you have to do for that day.

OK, so right now you're working on Day 2. Now is the time to select your Ultimate Goal for this 30 Day Detox. As I said earlier, first look at the five things you would like to improve or change about yourself; look at yourself from the inside. What are the little things that make your soul cringe? What makes your soul happy? Now once you have all those things down, you need to think of an ultimate goal. By achieving the smaller goals you will eventually reach your ultimate goal.

Use whatever came to you yesterday or earlier today. (You can do this 30 Day Detox over and over, so don't sweat over this first goal.) Make a note on Day 30 of what you would like to achieve this time. Put a date to it. So for me it was about forgiving people and allowing them to come into my life, for example: Day 30, August 21st - I will be able to attract more positive people in and let go of the negative influences in my life, and because of doing that I will achieve my networking goal and find someone to help me with my journey.

When you drive your car and are trying to reach your destination, you keep your eye on the end. You follow your GPS to take you in the right direction. If the freeway is jammed or there is construction on the road, we wait until we are able to move ahead. Yet in life we want to rush to our destinations jumping over minor setbacks. Instead, keep your destination in mind and deal with what comes up and then continue to move on.

Notice how the first two days are connected. The first day you began to get in touch with your smaller goals and look for the ultimate goal and the second day you selected it and put a date to the day you will achieve your goal. You might be thinking, "This is impossible... how can I achieve this?" But the truth is you can. You might achieve 100% of your goal, but even if you are at 60% there is still major improvement.

By keeping the end in mind, you know your Ultimate Goal. You aren't just scrambling in the dark, not knowing where to go and what you want. I would do that a lot; I longed for something bigger and better, but what was it? I had no clue. When I started writing, I realized that I could write 8 to 10 hours a day and not feel tired or stressed. At that point, I knew that was one of my major goals – to write and touch people's lives. But it wasn't easy. In order to help others, I had to help myself first and so I had to detox my soul! As you move through this book, you'll be detoxing your soul also, and this will support you as you work on your Ultimate Goal. So remember when you write down your notes for each day to include how you're doing with your Ultimate Goal.

NOTES

Day 2

NOTES

_____

_____

_____

_____

_____

_____

_____

_____

_____

_____

_____

_____

_____

_____

Day 3

Use Your Imagination

*O*nce you know what you want and where you want to be, start imagining yourself in that place or as that person. For me, I imagined myself having the characteristics of Mother Teresa, Maya Angelou and Nelson Mandela. Let me tell you why. I wanted to be kind, compassionate and nonjudgmental like Mother Teresa, I wanted to have the positive genuine soul of Maya Angelou, and of course I wanted to be able to stand up for what I believe just like Nelson Mandela did. I have never met any of these people in real life, but I strived to be like them. I admired their qualities rather than the person, as I feel that one of the biggest problems in our society is that we idolize people who are in the public eye. We treat them like they are above and beyond human.

So try to find certain characteristics in yourself that are holding you back from achieving that goal. Maybe you don't stand up to the bullies in your life, or you allow people to take undue advantage of you, or when success comes close, you step back instead of jumping forward. So jump in now! Close your eyes and see how you want to see yourself. This is actually a difficult thing to do. As human beings, we are scared to feel the greatness within us. So we stay in the form of a mediocre person, someone that we are OK being. Meanwhile, our biggest struggle is trying to move toward being someone who is way and above our very own expectations. The Universe knows we can achieve this, when will we find out?

So go crazy with your imagination! Do you want to see yourself as the best mom ever, or helping babies in Africa, or meeting the Queen of England, or adopting underprivileged children who need a good home, or even just being a great friend? Please don't confine yourself today; the bigger you dream, the closer you are to achieving it. Remember: Your reality is only as big as your dreams!

When I first started teaching, the biggest shock I had was when I asked my students, "Imagine that you are on the moon..." and a few students raised their hands before I could finish my sentence. So I stopped mid-sentence and said, "Yes?" One student asked, "I'm not on the moon, so how do I know what it's like?" That was such a sad and eye-opening moment for me. How can our children not know how to imagine? Even as adults, this is something we need to learn to do better and well. So imagine things that are outrageous, crazy and spectacular, because they might just come true!!

NOTES

_____

_____

_____

_____

_____

_____

_____

_____

_____

_____

_____

_____

_____

_____

_____

NOTES

_____

_____

_____

_____

_____

_____

_____

_____

_____

_____

_____

_____

_____

_____

Day 4

EXPLAIN THE GRATITUDE

This is something we have all heard before... to be grateful for what you have and to keep a gratitude journal. For years, I had done this, but one day as I was looking back at my journal I realized something. I saw that I had written things down, and now I couldn't remember the reason. I was feeling down, and one of my previous entries said, "I am thankful for a stranger." I wanted to know and remember what that stranger had done, but I just couldn't recall.

I decided that it was important to explain my gratitude, for the days I was just not feeling thankful. That way, I could be inspired by something from the past.

So, from then on, every time I would write, "I am thankful for..." I included a reason why. For example, I went for a walk one day and the sky was absolutely gorgeous. It was like the Divine Creator had sat there and painted a perfect morning. So I came back home and wrote, "I am thankful for a beautiful sky. I was lucky to witness the bluest of blue skies and the perfection of the clouds in their formation and color. I am also thankful that I decided to go for a walk today."

If you haven't already started a gratitude journal, I suggest you do so. I bought a nice journal to write in, but if you don't want to do that, just get a notebook. But try to find an attractive one, so it invites you to write in it. Then remember to write down the things that you are grateful for. Pick five things every day, but the catch is that they have to be different each day. Also, remember to write why you are thankful for those things. It will definitely brighten up your day when you look back after a few months or even years and realize how small random things are so important.

We have a tendency to run after the big promotion or the lotto win, but our gratitude journals are filled with a smile from a stranger, or time spent with family and friends, or even just looking up at the sky. So today and every day look at the small things in life that give you joy and make you smile. With technology at the tip of my fingers, I have started to put things on the notepad of my iPhone during the day. So when I sit down to write in my gratitude journal, I haven't forgotten anything at all!

Explain the Gratitude

NOTES

_____

_____

_____

_____

_____

_____

_____

_____

_____

_____

_____

_____

_____

_____

_____

_____

Day 4

NOTES

_____

_____

_____

_____

_____

_____

_____

_____

_____

_____

_____

_____

_____

_____

Day 5

Slash the Demon – Anger

This exercise is one of the hardest things I have done in my life. So I felt that it was best to get it over with at the beginning of the detox, as I wanted you to be able to practice this for the rest of the month.

Anger, in my opinion, is one of the worst emotions a human can have. People insult, hurt and even kill in a rage of anger. I feel that anger is such a superficial emotion. It comes and goes like the waves of the ocean. It comes and it can cause hell in someone's life. However, once it's gone, you can look back and realize that you had overreacted.

This exercise is also one of my favorites. It allowed me to see that I had so much hidden anger towards so many things and that I was in total denial about it. Once I figured out my hidden demons and what was pulling me down, I decided to slash those demons.

For me personally, I had so much anger which I hid inside. I appeared to be a calm collected person, but once something from the past would trigger my anger I would just fall into a depression. For years, I had this silent killer in me without even knowing it. It was time now to become my own Knight in Shining Armor and slash those inner demons.

So I sat down for my morning session and closed my eyes, and I chose to question my anger. I asked myself what were the things that made me angry, in the past and in the present. After I started to get my answers, I opened my eyes and wrote them down no matter how many tears fell. I continued to write everything I remembered that angered me – the people, the moments, the emotions and even the sights. It was really difficult as my anger rose and fell, but I had no one else to blame for keeping that inside of me.

Once I was a bit calmer, I then blessed every person and moment that had caused these negative feelings in me. I said, "I bless you my ex-friend even though you made me angry." By blessing it, I removed the poison that was flowing in my veins and changed it into love and forgiveness. I had never before tried to get rid of negative feelings and replace them with positive ones, and believe me, I felt physically lighter when I did. It was like I weighed less! I felt like someone had removed a huge rock from my brain.

Today, take 20 minutes of your time to do this. You are slashing your demons with love. It's not an easy exercise but take my word for it this will change your life. Bless your demons every single day during this 30 day detox. You don't have to write down your demons every day, only today. On the days that follow, close your eyes and bless whatever demons come to your mind. It could even be an event that happened that day and isn't on your list.

NOTES

_____

_____

_____

_____

_____

_____

_____

_____

_____

_____

_____

_____

_____

_____

_____

_____

NOTES

Day 6

REIN IN THE RESENTMENT

Resentment is something that most people-pleasers deal with. We tend to keep the needs of others ahead of our own. In our tendency to make the world a happier place, we forget ourselves. Then, later on, when we realize that others don't do the same or our needs aren't reciprocated, we resent the other people and the world.

I did that for most of my life and it was extremely painful. There were days when I felt physically in pain, because the internal pain was so much. One day, I realized that I needed to get rid of the past resentments and live for today and look forward.

I sat down in a comfortable position and first wrote down what I resented most – for me, it was just not being able to stand up to the bullies in my life. So I wrote that down. Then I closed my eyes and visualized myself sitting with each one of these bullies. I told them nicely that I was handing back all the resentment that I had towards them and that I forgave them. I wasn't able to do this in one sitting so I spread it out over the day. I did one bully at a time. By the end of the day, I felt so light and like a feather. It was so liberating and exciting. I did eventually come face-to-face with one of these people I had identified as a bully, and after this exercise, I saw her as weak and vulnerable. I wasn't threatened by her in anyway, which interestingly caused her to back off.

Day 6

Today is your day to do the same, to liberate yourself from these resentments. No matter what they are and who is causing it. Know that the other person, just like you, is trying to do their best and live their life to the fullest! They possibly are even more scared then you are.

NOTES

_____

_____

_____

_____

_____

_____

_____

_____

_____

_____

_____

_____

_____

_____

_____

_____

NOTES

_____

_____

_____

_____

_____

_____

_____

_____

_____

_____

_____

_____

_____

_____

_____

_____

Day 7

FACE THE FEAR

Today is your day to face your fears. By fear, I don't mean the fear of heights or jumping out of an airplane, but the fear of a worst case scenario. You might fear for the future, fear facing someone who you've been feuding with, fear being great, or even maybe just fear living life to the fullest. But this needs to stop, because the truth is that fear (like anger) is just an emotion that comes and goes. Fear is what truthfully holds us back from being the greatest person that we can be.

Unfortunately, a lot of women today have a fear of spending their lives alone, so they settle for the wrong kind of guy – someone who abuses them. For these readers, I say learn to be with yourself, to be your own best companion.

For myself, what I did was that I actually sat down and created an image of my worst case scenario. I can't draw to save my life, but it was a fun experience to try. I actually also cut out pictures from magazines and created an anti-dream board – things I feared and didn't want to deal with in the future. I made my beautiful board, laughed while doing it, and smiled at the things I feared and it became a fun experience.

Once I was done, I took a good look at all the things on my board and then I ripped it up. I ripped it into a hundred pieces and threw it away. It was such a relief. I had looked the things I feared in the eyes and I actually made a little fun activity out of facing them. Eventually I ripped up every fear I had into lots of pieces. So there was nothing left to fear! After that day, whenever fear crept up on me, I would go back and remember that day and it would get me past the fear.

Today I urge you to do the same. If you don't have time to cut out pictures, just draw a funny picture of you and your fears, laugh about it, and then rip it all up. Believe me, it's really fun!!

NOTES

_____

_____

_____

_____

_____

_____

_____

_____

_____

_____

_____

_____

_____

_____

_____

_____

_____

Day 7

NOTES

28

Day 8

DREAM AND SMILE

I have a dear friend of mine who has been instrumental in helping me through this journey that we call "Life." Every time I would be stressed, my dear friend would say, "Dream and smile." It never made sense to me because, at those moments in my life, I was too busy being negative and grumpy.

When I embarked on my detox journey, I was looking back at my old journals and found this phrase – *dream and smile*. All of a sudden, it made sense! I needed to dream my biggest dream and believe that the Universe would assist me in fulfilling it.

So I wrote down my dream; it was a simple one – I wanted to be able to write and be appreciated for what I was writing. Once I wrote my dream, I smiled every time I thought about it. The thought just illuminated my heart. I had turned it over to the Universe to make it happen, and miraculously before my 30 day detox was over, I became an official blogger for *The Huffington Post!* It was unbelievable. I had been working as a teacher for the past 12 years and this opportunity just opened up for me. I knew that this wasn't my final destination, but it was the beginning of my soul's journey to meet the greatness that I was created for.

So dream big, smile about your dream, and have faith in the Universe. You will notice that your dream will mirror your ultimate goal in so many ways, it might even be the same. Dreams can come true!! Think about your dream at least two to three times a day. It doesn't have to be a long intense thought. As you're driving, sitting at your desk, or even in the shower, just think of your dream and how you would feel when you achieve it! Don't forget to smile!

By the way, I have always been a dreamer. My favorite pastime used to be to dream about random crazy things. Dreamers like me are never at the top of their class. We are constantly dreaming of a how and what to create. It could be in the form of putting words, colors, lines, jewelry, fabric, etc. together to create a masterpiece. People like Einstein, Beethoven, Thomas Edison, Mary Shelley, Walt Disney, James Cameron and many more took their dreams and made it into their reality. So today become a dreamer and allow your biggest most beautiful dream to come out!

NOTES

NOTES

_____

_____

_____

_____

_____

_____

_____

_____

_____

_____

_____

_____

_____

_____

_____

_____

Day 9

Navigate Your Soul

The Sufi poet Rumi said:

"When you do things from your soul,
you feel a river moving in you, a joy."

The reason why I keep on using the word "soul" is because I personally feel that our soul is our authentic self. How we dress, where we live, how we spend our time each day, and our hobbies are all part of our physical being. However, the things we feel in our hearts – like when you see a child laugh or when you do something that you were meant to do – automatically you are talking to your soul.

My dear friend Ghazala, who is a Montessori teacher, told me that she loves being around children in a Montessori environment. It's like her heart is just simply happy and content. That is when you know that you are aligned with your purpose in life.

A lot of people feel that when they're in a relationship, their heart sings and their soul is happy. I feel that it's not because they are in "love," but because this person fills in some hole in our soul. But we can also do this for ourselves, by listening to our own soul.

I have been a teacher for the past 12 years. I am good at what I do and I enjoy teaching 5th and 6th graders. I have been a homeroom teacher and teach all core subjects. However, when I'm teaching the children how to write creatively, my heart starts beating a little faster and I get so excited. Even my students' notice how my eyes open up wider and my smile gets bigger – this is what I mean.

Start noticing the small things that make your heart smile. If it's taking pictures of nature, then do more of it. If it's preparing healthy meals, then spend time doing that. Navigate your soul towards what you love to do. Feel the little "text messages" that your soul sends you. Listen when your soul tells you not to jump into something and navigate your soul towards the things that make your heart smile.

Take the reins of your life and steer it towards your inner greatness. Don't be shy. You can achieve anything if you don't stop in the middle and stay persistent. You will go through turns and twists, but eventually you will get there. Use your soul as your personal GPS; notice what makes it happy and content. Spend *at least* 10% of your time doing that. Slowly increase that time and it will make you a happier person.

NOTES

_____

_____

_____

_____

_____

_____

_____

_____

_____

_____

_____

_____

_____

_____

_____

_____

_____

NOTES

_____

_____

_____

_____

_____

_____

_____

_____

_____

_____

_____

_____

_____

_____

_____

_____

_____

Day 10

Say Cheese!

I know when you see the simple title of this chapter, you might roll your eyes and think, and "I've heard that before!" But please hear me out. I have done this myself, days when I was feeling down or depressed. I would force myself to smile at everyone, the guy at the grocery store, the random person crossing the street while I was in my car, or even a neighbor. It definitely lifted my spirits. I don't know how or why, but it absolutely did! And so much research is out there that would prove my point.

This topic reminds me of an acquaintance of mine, who is a teacher. She had a habit of always smiling. Every time I would run into her, she would give me a gigantic genuine smile and say, "Hi!" It was nice some days, but other days I felt annoyed about her cheerful outlook on life. So many times when I was feeling down, I would become irritated when she would repeatedly greet me with a smile.

Finally I asked her how she could always be so happy. Her answer changed my life forever. She told me (with a smile, of course), "Honey, that's the only thing I have left to fight this cancer with. Chemo and radiation aren't strong enough to get rid of those cancer cells, but a positive attitude is."

If that teacher can muster up a warm smile, so can you! Remember to smile a bit more today; laugh at small things. Some of our best memories are of when we laugh at silly things with friends or family.

Some days when I'm feeling extra down and someone will smile at me, it makes so much of a difference in my whole day. So fill your soul with the simple joy of brightening up someone's day with a smile and it will also help your soul – no matter how broken it is. Meanwhile, you'll be filling the cells of your body with positive energy!!

NOTES

_____

_____

_____

_____

_____

_____

_____

_____

_____

_____

_____

_____

_____

_____

_____

_____

NOTES

Day 11

JUST BREATHE!

Today's exercise is a little difficult. It was hard for me because I'm a person who enjoys controlling things. I like things to be done on time and I worry about "What's next?" I know I need to relax, but I never use to allow myself to do it. That is until one fine day when my 13-year-old son Usman told me, "Mom, just breathe. It's OK if you don't finish cooking on time, we don't have dinner by 6:30."

Of course I said, "How can you say that? Everything needs to be done on time!" However, it got me thinking. Why do I feel that I need to rush through life? Since I'm a person who likes to have a set schedule, letting things slip off my time table and being relaxed about it was really hard.

Yet life is going to pass us by, no matter what. Isn't it better to stop, breathe and enjoy?

Your exercise for Day 11 is to stop and breathe. When you feel like you're hurrying and rushing like crazy, just stop yourself and look around. Is there something that you're missing? Maybe your child is unhappy, or your dog needs a little extra loving, or it might even be you that needs some tender loving care. So just STOP every time you're rushing and breathe. Sit down if you're standing up... stop if you're walking fast... and just breathe. (But don't stop the car in the middle of the road if you're driving!)

It's absolutely OK if dinner is at 6:40 or 7 PM instead of 6:30, believe me. I learned from my child that dinner is absolutely fine if it's a little late. It's being together to share the meal that counts!

NOTES

_____

_____

_____

_____

_____

_____

_____

_____

_____

_____

_____

_____

_____

_____

_____

_____

_____

NOTES

Day 12

PRAY LIKE THERE'S NO TOMORROW

Prayer is not asking. It is a longing of the soul.
It is daily admission of one's weakness.
It is better in prayer to have a heart without words
than words without a heart."
– Mahatma Gandhi

Prayer has always been a powerful tool in most religions. Each of these religions has a prescribed way of praying, which is a part of their daily ritual. Prayer is usually considered to be a ritual that is performed to ask a higher power for something.

I look at prayer differently, I talk to God. I talk to him like he is my best friend. I joke with God and I argue with him. I talk to him while driving, eating dinner, and during my work as a teacher. And when I'm meditating, I become one with a higher power. In meditation, I truly feel at peace with whatever is going on in my life.

Today, find a place where you can sit comfortably. It actually doesn't have to be a place of utter silence or a perfect environment. You can pray very well in a place where the world is running around you. Just find a place to sit as this is a very powerful exercise.

Close your eyes and imagine that you're in the midst of a beautiful garden filled with light. Your soul is there and so is your Creator. Talk to him. Tell him how you feel... that some days you feel let down... or thank him for giving you so many blessings.

I try to always start with a "Thank you!" and slowly my complaints just go away. After I'm done saying what I had to say, I quietly say, "Amen," and open my eyes. Most days it's like I'm going into a trance and I come out feeling a lot lighter and happier. And why wouldn't I? I am talking to the Creator who loves me more than I can love myself.

I don't believe that God is only in a place of worship. I feel him everywhere around me – in my darkest days and in my best moments. So today write about your conversation with Him, what did you thank Him for? What did you complain about?

NOTES

_____

_____

_____

_____

_____

_____

_____

_____

_____

_____

_____

_____

_____

_____

_____

Day 12

NOTES

48

Day 13

TELL THE WORLD!

A lot of times when we tell the people we love that we're moving towards improving our lives or following our dreams, for some reason their reaction is weird. Either we get a response of "Mmmm... OK... well, good luck!" or they give us a discouraging look. Very few people will say, "I'm so proud of you... go for it!"

Being a people-pleaser, it was really difficult to accept that not a lot of people were happy for me when I decided to follow my dreams. Everyone around me knew what I had been through to reach that point in my life. My whole life I told everyone I was a writer, and I would get "the look." How could they not know how everything in my life was pointing towards this time?

One day I was up early in the morning doing my meditation. I couldn't stop crying and complaining to myself about how the world wasn't as excited as I was about my dream and how could people be so heartless, etc. And then it dawned on me... everyone has their own destiny to reach. People were happy for me but they really didn't know how much this meant to me. So I started telling more people. I even announced it on my Facebook page, which basically meant that there was no turning back. I asked people for their blessings and prayers, and the good wishes started pouring in.

Day 13

I truly believe that when you put your deepest intentions out there to the world, the Universe in turn will shower you with blessings. So, today, tell the people you meet what you plan to do and say it with conviction. If you want it happen, it will! Believe in your destiny and be proud of yourself. Also write down the reaction you get from people, it will give you joy the days when you need it.

NOTES

NOTES

Day 14

BECOME A STUDENT

When we hear the word "student," we automatically think of someone enrolled in a school, a college or a university... usually someone in their youth. However, this is a total misconception. We still need to keep learning as we get older. If we are continuing to evolve, learning is a constant in our lives. As Socrates said:

"Education is the kindling of a flame, not the filling of a vessel."

We can never have enough knowledge. Learn things every day. Learn how to soar from the bird, how to be determined from the fly. (A tiny fly can annoy the hell out of you. No matter what you do, it is determined to continue to buzz around.)

A young child can teach you how to just be yourself and be free. It's amazing to see children playing in a playground. They will jump and make funny sounds and faces, but that's what they are feeling in that moment.

Continue to learn from everything around you. No matter how academically educated you are, the world is such a huge, beautiful and mysterious place – just like our soul.

I learned this lesson in a very interesting way. There was a time in my life when I was very down. I complained about everything and I mean *everything.* One day, I decided to go for a walk. Along the way, I saw a humming bird. This bird was just randomly flying up and down next to a flower. I was totally mesmerized and I decided to just sit out-side of someone's house and watch the humming bird.

As I sat there and observed, the humming bird just continued to fly in its distinct way. I didn't understand why, but all of a sudden tears started to run down my face. It was like I was given a message. This tiny bird didn't care who was watching her, if the world was just pass-ing by her, or what anyone would do to her. She was busy doing what the Divine had created her to do.

I later did research and found out that humming birds are loners. They prefer to be alone – just the way I used to be. But this bird was content and happy, instead of worrying about tomorrow. At that point, I – the big arrogant human being – was so humbled by the confidence and faith of this little bird. I believe that bird was there to teach me a lesson in faith and in believing in myself.

Today, feel like a student of life. Tell yourself that you will learn from everything – from something as big as a human being all the way to something as tiny as a fly. Open your eyes and your ears today, and allow Life to teach and embrace you!

NOTES

NOTES

_____

_____

_____

_____

_____

_____

_____

_____

_____

_____

_____

_____

_____

_____

_____

_____

_____

Day 15

MEDITATE

I'm sure you must be wondering why I brought in the topic of meditation halfway through this detox journey. There is a reason for that. A lot of cleansing needs to be done before meditation can be practiced properly.

Learning how to meditate in the right way took me a long time to get. I had always heard people talk about how meditation changed their lives. We all want to do this, but has anyone really taught us how to meditate correctly?

I wanted to be like the people in the movies who look so peaceful and perfect while meditating. For the first few days, I just couldn't do it! Still, I continued to try every day. I sat in the yoga pose and closed my eyes. It just didn't work for me.

With my thunder thighs, it had been difficult to sit comfortably in the cross-legged yoga pose. My breakthrough came when I thought of an alternative – sitting outside on a comfortable chair in my backyard. So it was just me seated on my chair, and I tilted my head back and closed my eyes. I tried to focus on myself and started to breathe in and out. I just listened to myself breathing and thoughts came, but I would turn my focus back to my breathing. Slowly all my other random thoughts started to fade away.

I'm serious, it was like a miracle. Meditation began to work for me! I started with sitting there for as long as I could until I just had to open my eyes. It began with 3 minutes and I am now up to 30 minutes a day.

I have really pondered upon why meditation is such a powerful tool in soul healing. Ironically enough, I actually figured it out during meditation. It's because we are silent and at peace within ourselves. A place of not feeling anger, hurt or pain can be reached during meditation, because we're not struggling to be perfect for the world. We aren't feeling guilty for not achieving desired goals, and we aren't feeling like we are unlucky or were treated unjustly.

All we are doing during meditation is becoming one with ourselves. We aren't judging ourselves or others; we are content with being one with the Universe. That, in reality, is what our souls long for.

So your assignment today is to meditate in the traditional way or just find a quiet place, close your eyes and listen to yourself breathe – that soft rhythmic sound that is in perfect harmony. Some days when I'm really into my meditation, I can even hear or feel the soft thumping of my heart beat.

Start meditating every day, even if you don't know how to do it correctly. Continue to try and eventually feel how perfectly you were created!

NOTES

NOTES

Day 16

The Best Day of My Life!

This is a practice that I have begun, and it really does have an interesting impact on my life. What I do is, after my morning meditation every day; I tell myself that "Today is going to be the best day of my life!" I repeat this a few times – no matter how bad I feel (some days were so bad that I wanted to just stop).

However, there were days that positive things started to happen or maybe I began to notice the good things. I started to write again, and people enjoyed what I wrote. I went to a great Lionel Richie concert. I had my laser eye surgery done (I hadn't been able to see with my own eyes for the past 30+ years). I started to write this book, met some cool positive people, and just enjoyed every day.

This worked for me because instead of dreading the day ahead I was actually excited about it. I was looking for exciting things that were happening to me during the day. It totally changed my whole persona. I am now happy to be alive and living.

So, starting with Day 16, tell yourself every day that "Today is going to be the best day of my life" and it truly will. Sure, there will be days when you will wake up feeling blah and think, "No, today is going to be a difficult day." But stop yourself right there and repeat after me: "Even though I'm feeling grumpy and tired, I will still have the best day of my life. I will not let my initial mood take away the joy that I will find today." Say and write this three times. Miracles will happen!!

I promise you that you'll have a great day!

The Best Day of My Life!

NOTES

Day 16

NOTES

Day 17

PAST, PRESENT AND FUTURE

I used to be intimidated and intrigued by three friends of mine, these friends were my past, present and future. At the same time, I realized that my *past* had molded me – like a piece of clay – into the person that I am. I can't hate it because this made me the person who loves to write, who can feel other people's pain, who gets angry at unfairness, and a lot more. How can I not like what my past has done for me? I needed the past that I was given to reach my Ultimate Path that the Universe had chosen for me.

My *future* is also not an evil demon. I've realized that it's what gives me my dreams, aspirations, my wings to fly, the reason to wake up, and the excitement to see my children grow up and become good people. How can I even be human if I have no dreams? In my all-time favorite book, *The Alchemist* by Paulo Coehlo, the crystal merchant (one of the characters) refuses to fulfill his dream because if he does that what would he have to live for?

And what can I say about the *present?* It's every single breath we take, every time our heart beats, when we feel a certain emotion, when our heart sinks for someone else who is in pain, or when we laugh so much we cry. It is the complete beautiful second that we have because every cell in our body is working in perfect harmony, just like the Universe and nature does. It is a culmination of what has made me and of what I will achieve in the future. That tiny moment that we call "the present" is all that we have to create a beautiful past and future.

So, today, remember to not fear or resent these three – the past, present and future – but appreciate what they have done for you. Love your *past* for making you the wonderful person you are. Enjoy your *present*, for if you give your all to it, you will have an awesome *future!* Think of them as your allies. Write about what the past has given you to make you who you are, what you want the future to hold for you, and how you will make the most of the present!

NOTES

Day 17

NOTES

_____

_____

_____

_____

_____

_____

_____

_____

_____

_____

_____

_____

_____

_____

_____

_____

Day 18

BE HUMBLE AND FORGIVE

*I*f you ask me, one of the biggest plagues that affect the human race is arrogance. We are all readily available to criticize others for their actions, but hardly any of us put ourselves in the shoes of another person. Today, your assignment is to sit down and think of up to five people who you feel have hurt you mentally and emotionally. Select people who you feel really wronged you. Once you have written their names down, try to separate your own ego from that situation where they hurt you and think, "What were they going through themselves at that time? Why would they be mean to me? Was it something from their past?" It's very difficult to do this because our natural ego usually jumps in. But please trust me and just do it – no matter how awful it makes you feel.

After this exercise, you will actually feel empathy for these people. Know that there is also the issue of karma, of which I am a true believer. If there is someone out there who hurt you intentionally and knowingly, believe me they will suffer the guilt.

A few years ago, I was feeling very sad about something someone had done to intentionally hurt me, and a wise friend of mine said, "Don't worry about it. Remember that if we treat people with kindness and compassion we are in heaven, because we are at peace with our actions. However, if we treat people with distrust and arrogance, that's when we create our own hell. It's our choice to either allow our mind to live in heaven or hell. She (the person who had hurt me) will get whatever she chooses."

To me, that was such a liberating thought. To know that there is a force bigger than me that will question everyone – including myself – on our actions. That force is not some super power but our own souls.

So remember to give the world positive energy and be humble so that's what you will get in return! For me to be humble and kind enough to forgive this person, I'm sure forgiveness will come back to me. Today catch your arrogant ego when it tries to pull you down.

NOTES

_____

_____

_____

_____

_____

_____

_____

_____

_____

_____

_____

_____

_____

_____

_____

_____

Day 18

NOTES

_____

_____

_____

_____

_____

_____

_____

_____

_____

_____

_____

_____

_____

_____

_____

_____

Day 19

LISTEN TO YOU

*A*lways remember to listen to the little voice inside of you. Our soul knows what is right and what is wrong. I like to call it "our text messages to God" and I believe he will always reply. If we listen to the little voice which we also call "intuition," all the answers are there. We know when we are wrong and we know when we are on our real path.

I have had issues with this; growing up, I was a not-so-confident person. I followed what others said instead of listening to my heart. But I knew that whenever I wrote, I was the happiest. In my heart of hearts, I always told myself that I was a writer. But I chose to not listen to that voice and became a teacher. I enjoyed teaching, but it wasn't my calling. I refused to listen to my intuition on so many different occasions and suffered the consequences.

So, today, sit down quietly and figure out what your intuition is trying to tell you. Is it telling you to call someone who you haven't spoken to in years, or is telling you to apply for that job, or maybe you need to change your diet as you are struggling with your health? Make sure that every day you listen to that tiny voice inside that tells you that you're the best. The voice that gives you the map to your greatness, it is in you, believe me!

Before I started this book, I was desperately looking to change careers from teaching to curriculum development. However, every time I started looking, I would get distracted and start thinking about my book. That's when I realized that my destiny wasn't to have another career; it was to write my heart out and let the world know what I had learned.

Remember... you have all the answers – *just listen!!* Sometimes when you're about to make a decision, just sit with it and think about what your real inner self is saying.

NOTES

NOTES

_____

_____

_____

_____

_____

_____

_____

_____

_____

_____

_____

_____

_____

_____

_____

_____

Day 20

SEEK SOLITUDE

$\mathcal{S}$olitude is one of the biggest weapons a human being has. Here's the reason. When you're alone, that's when you can face your demons, fight your addictions, and learn to love yourself. The biggest punishment for a crime is usually solitary confinement because being with you is also the most difficult thing to do. When you're with yourself, you see the ugliness and the beauty and that is the time when you can get rid of the ugliness and convert it back into a masterpiece.

I believe we were born perfect, the way we are meant to be – pure and innocent. During this journey – from our first breath to our last – it is only solitude that keeps us sane and connected with our soul. I can very honestly say that having my solitude is what has saved me many times from losing myself.

So, each day, remember to take some time to be with yourself. This doesn't mean while watching TV or reading. It means just sitting alone, thinking and evaluating what you're doing right and what you're doing wrong in your life. Think about your journey of life and how you could enhance it. One of my mentors once said, "The essence of life is in being with you."

I know how busy our lives have become and how difficult it is to take a few minutes out for ourselves. Believe me, it's there somewhere. It might be when you're in the car waiting to pick up your kids, or at work at your desk, or even right before going to bed. Carve out time to be with YOU!

Today, find at least 15 minutes to be alone, without the television, your phone, or any other device – not even a book or a magazine. Just be with yourself. Write down some things you really like about yourself – bravery, humor, and your logical mind, whatever it is.

NOTES

Day 20

NOTES

Day 21

FILL UP YOUR ACCOUNTS

A dear wise friend of mine named Star, who is an energy healer and an acupuncturist, told me, "Your body is like your savings account. The more you put in, the more you will get out, if you put in junk – which can include junk food or junk thoughts – that's what you will get out." So if you want to live a good authentic life, you need to fill up your physical, mental, spiritual and emotional accounts.

Star told me this at a time of my life when I was feeling extremely low, and my health had suffered tremendously. Life had brought me to a point where I just didn't want to do anything. I was like a robot; I would wake up, go to work, come back and just do my chores. I was emotionally dead. However, thanks to my friend Star, I began to fill up my accounts!

Remember, as far as your body is concerned, if you put in junk food and no exercise, you will suffer. These behaviors will eventually create a body that has health issues.

Start by doing one healthy thing for yourself. For the next week, eat an extra piece of fruit or an additional serving of vegetables instead of that bag of chips. The week after, increase it slowly. It might take you three months to change even 50% of your diet, but eventually you'll be able to replace all the junk food. If you have a sedentary lifestyle, start walking for only 10 minutes every day.

While I was growing up, my mother was always very active and took good care of herself. When she wasn't able to get her exercise done during the day, she would walk in front of the TV while watching programs in the evening. She would walk back and forth and get her 10 to 15 minutes of exercise that way. So be creative!

Believe me, this has been difficult for me. For one, I love everything fried. In addition, I hate exercising. I'd rather sit on my bed and read for 10 hours than go to the gym for 30 minutes. So I started with walking, and now I can walk up to 5 miles a day and I'm starting to run. My goal is to be able to run those 5 miles. I did it very slowly and it took me three months to go from 10 minutes to 5 miles. Now I walk on the treadmill or ride the stationary bike at the gym while reading!

As far as your thoughts are concerned, every time you get a negative, self-demeaning thought, stop yourself. Take a deep breath and think something nice about yourself. Just do it! Every time you have a negative thought, counter it with something nice. Eventually, your brain will be trained to do it on its own. The junk thoughts will be substituted by positive thoughts. This will help your self-esteem and your relationships with others. I know it helped me!

Today, feed yourself one healthy food, do one simple exercise, and think one good thought! Write down the changes you plan to make. Slowly increase these and fill up your accounts with good food, regular exercise, and soul-worthy thoughts!

NOTES

Day 21

NOTES

_____

_____

_____

_____

_____

_____

_____

_____

_____

_____

_____

_____

_____

_____

_____

Day 22

LOVE THE BEAUTY

Today is the day to spread the love. First, you're going to give some to yourself. Just be happy to be the person you were made to be. You might not be feeling so grateful – maybe you're depressed, maybe you lost someone dear to you – but, please, I still urge you to feel beautiful and proud. So many people have lost their lives that were a lot younger than we are. We were given this life to find the beauty in every minute thing. First and foremost, we need to find it in ourselves.

Today, I want you to sit in front of the mirror and take a look at yourself. What is there that you find beautiful? Start with small things. Do you have nice hair? Do you like the color? How about the shape of your face or the arch in your eyebrows? What about your eyes? Do they show kindness? Are they nicely shaped? Your smile – is it genuine? How about your neck, hands and feet... what do you like about them? Look at every part of you and find five things that are just amazing. Don't be so judgmental of yourself. We are all perfect and whole in our own way.

One of my students once said to me, "Ms. Tami, we all have beautiful and perfect hearts when we are born. But for mean people, the ugliness slowly comes from their heart to their face. That's why people don't look beautiful after a while." So remember the beauty of a perfect heart and soul ends up showing on our faces! Our good deeds improve our looks... what a thought! It's not the wrinkle-free botoxed face or perfect body, but kindness that brightens up the world. Audrey Hepburn was a true example of this. Her kindness and good heart shone through in her looks. Fill up your heart with love and it will be reflected in a beautiful way in your appearance.

NOTES

_____

_____

_____

_____

_____

_____

_____

_____

_____

_____

_____

_____

_____

_____

_____

NOTES

_____

_____

_____

_____

_____

_____

_____

_____

_____

_____

_____

_____

_____

_____

_____

_____

_____

Day 23

Be Aware

I was lucky enough to attend a lecture by Byron Katie in Ojai, California. If you haven't read her books, you really need to check them out. I drove up there alone. It was about two to three hours away from where I live.

As she walked on stage, I saw a beautiful woman who just exuded positive energy. Unfortunately, a half an hour into her talk, I ran out sobbing and drove home. Back home, I felt extremely overwhelmed and restless. I wasn't able to sleep that night and many nights afterwards.

Byron Katie makes people aware of their feelings and emotions – of their worst demons. She tells people we assume that what other people say about us is actually how we feel about ourselves. She forced me just through her talk to be aware of the negativity that was inside of me. I was blaming others for my own shortcomings and my unhappiness. We do that so easily as humans. For example, we blame our parents for who we have become as adults. However, the truth is that we are adults now, and it is our choice to change ourselves according to what we want.

Day 23 is the day to become aware, to look within. Look back at the worst moments of your life, and think of what you did and what the other person did. Was it really 100% the other person's fault? Sometimes it is, but most of the time it isn't.

You don't need to discuss this with anyone, but be aware of the mental trap that you put yourself in when someone pushes your buttons or begins to lead you in a bad direction. At those times, you can blame the other person so much that they become the demon in your life. However, maybe you're wrong? I'm not saying that you are, but take a look inside. It's disturbing but sometimes what's happening in our life is the result of our own assumptions and beliefs.

Become aware of who your real demons are, because they do reside within. Write down five demons that pull you down. Next time someone tries to draw you into a bad situation or presents you in a bad light, see your part or your own perspective and don't participate. You don't have to fall into the same old traps!

NOTES

NOTES

_____

_____

_____

_____

_____

_____

_____

_____

_____

_____

_____

_____

_____

_____

_____

_____

_____

Day 24

BE AND LET BE

So what does this saying mean – "Be and let be"? It means to let things be the way they are. Sometimes we want to save a friend or a relative, but that person isn't willing to change. We take it upon ourselves to become the savior, however most of the time it backfires.

If you see someone who is suffering or needs you, go right ahead be there for them. Be a good listener and a compassionate friend. At the same time, remember that you can't make them change things for themselves.

Let me explain this through an example. A dear friend of mine was having major marital problems. She was there for me throughout my whole life and I wanted to be there for her. She told me what was going on and asked me what she should do. Of course, me being the "savior" that I was, I told her that she should leave him and began a new life. My friend was young and beautiful, and she had a great career and one child. I thought I was giving her the right advice.

After a few days when I didn't hear anything from her, I knew something was wrong. I waited for about a month and called her. She said that during a fight she told her husband that I thought it was best for her to leave him. Now that they were trying to work things out, her husband forbid her from seeing or talking to me. That was the end of our friendship. I still mourn the loss of my friend, but I learned a valuable lesson.

Today, look back for situations from the past when you overstepped your part and tried to be someone's savior. Recognize and write down the ways that this led to a bad result. Then, in the future, when you come to a point where someone wants you to save them, just step back and smile. Tell them you'll be there for emotional support, but you won't be making decisions for them or solving their problem.

There's another thing I want to mention about "Be and let be." Don't try to change everything around you. When we tend to do that, we are so busy living in the future that we forget about the beautiful present moments. Today, also write down what is perfect at this very moment that you're in, and enjoy it.

NOTES

NOTES

Day 25

EMBRACE

Today I want you to dress up. Even if you just planned to stay home or go grocery shopping – wear something nice. Wear something that makes you feel good. Research has proven that people feel much better about themselves if they practice good self-care.

Once you're already looking great, go out into the world and embrace the beauty that is called "the Universe." Do the activities you planned or just go for a walk, and embrace everything that comes your way. Take a deep breath and embrace the beautiful oxygen. Imagine that it's going into your lungs, into your blood and then spreading throughout your body, like a tiny tornado providing fuel and cleansing impurities as it goes. Look at the sky and embrace the sunlight or the clouds, and just smile at the thought of what these forces of nature are giving to you... how they're enhancing your life today.

Mentally embrace everyone that comes your way today. Embrace each person by acknowledging them and letting them know that you see that individual as a part of this beautiful Universe. When you give others the love that's hiding in your heart, that love will reflect on them and come straight back at you. Also, embrace the animals you see – the birds, butterflies, cats, dogs, etc.

Spend your day embracing and acknowledging the things around you. It will bring you to acknowledging and embracing yourself as well.

Day 25

Spend your time today embracing the Universe and the Universe will embrace you!! Write down 3-5 ways in which you have embraced the universe around you.

NOTES

NOTES

Day 26

Fun, Fun and More Fun

Today, just have fun! If you get a chance to observe children, please take the time to do that. Younger children will only think about doing things that give them pleasure. They don't care about who is watching them, all they want is to enjoy themselves. If you're a mother, you know we grow tired of hearing our kids say, "I want to do this and I want to go there." But I've realized that their insistence is because they understand the importance of enjoying themselves. My kids can drive me absolutely nuts when they really want to do something fun.

So today and everyday remember to enjoy your day and have fun. If you're like I was and life has taken you to a place where you don't even remember what you used to do for fun, then you absolutely need to find out. Today, write down the things that make you feel happy and free. Write down at least three activities. These should be things that make your heart sing and dance. When you do them, you can just be yourself and enjoy. Once you know what that is, make sure that you do one such activity every month. If you do it and realize that it doesn't make you happy anymore, find something else you want to do!

NOTES

Day 27

FORGIVE YOU!

*I*n order to find peace and move ahead in your life, you need to forgive yourself. As humans, we work so hard to do everything perfectly. We have to look great... need to have a perfect home, job and children. We blame ourselves if anything goes wrong, no matter how big or small. I know I set such high standards for myself, and I tend to get so disappointed when I don't get there. I haven't been able to forgive myself for things from 20 years ago, and I do feel that they're like shackles around my ankles and they just won't let me move on. This is something I'm still working on every day. I feel like being so hard on myself does hinder my success in so many ways.

So, today, just forgive things you did in the past – no matter how big or small. Be kind to yourself and allow yourself to grow. That can only come through forgiveness. I also feel that we hide the fact that we haven't forgiven ourselves so deep inside of us. We don't even let our conscious self know that we haven't forgiven ourselves.

Think today about whether there is something hiding in your heart that you're still angry with yourself over. Maybe it's falling in love with the wrong person, or not finishing your education, or becoming an alcoholic – even when your inner voice said, "Don't do it!" It's OK that you made those mistakes, but now is the time to move on and forgive yourself. Write those things down and face them, tell them yourself you are human and just trying to do your best!

Sometimes we aren't angry at others as much as we are with ourselves. So today look within and believe that you CAN be forgiven and go ahead and do it!

NOTES

_____

_____

_____

_____

_____

_____

_____

_____

_____

_____

_____

_____

_____

_____

_____

_____

NOTES

_____

_____

_____

_____

_____

_____

_____

_____

_____

_____

_____

_____

_____

_____

_____

_____

_____

Day 28

CREATE

Now that you've done most of the work, your assignment today is going to be lots of fun. I want you to create something – a piece of art, a meal, an article, a puppet or even just put together an outfit with pieces of clothing you have never paired before now. Although I love writing, I decided to create a building using Jenga blocks that was my piece of art. I also put a flower in my hair to create a different look.

So you have my permission to go wild and crazy with your creations (please do submit photos of what you created to my website tamishai-kh.com). I want you to notice how much love and kindness you put into making them. How would you feel if someone just walked by and carelessly broke or ruined it? In the same way, we were created in the purest form of love. Even more love than our hearts can take. We were not created to suffer, but we do.

Today, remember that you were created by the Divine in the best and purest form. You were created to love yourself and others. So enjoy that thought today. I have been reading about the Sufi philosophy, and they believe that the way we want God in our life is the same way He wants us to experience him. So think of your Creator and yourself with love. Write down your emotions while creating it and how you felt once your masterpiece was done.

NOTES

_____

_____

_____

_____

_____

_____

_____

_____

_____

_____

_____

_____

_____

_____

_____

_____

Day 29

TAKE IT ALL IN

Today is the day to take it all in. Go back and read the notes that you wrote. See if you feel better than when you started. You'll probably be shocked about some of the things that you wrote during the first few days. Look at those notes and reflect on how far you've come. Appreciate that you have been so honest with yourself and were able to come this far. Even if you weren't 100% honest, at least you were 60%, and that should be more than enough. You have progressed, even if it's just a little bit, so see this and appreciate it!

When you do decide to read your notes, remember to make sure you're sitting down and in a comfortable position. That you've selected a place where you can cry and laugh, mourn and rejoice the going of the Old You and the birth of the New You.

In addition, don't be so harsh on YOU. It's unrealistic to think you'll wake up and be a whole new person. It took you all these years to get to this stage of being the person you are, with your strengths and weaknesses. It will also take some time to undo the weaknesses and enhance the strengths.

So today write about what you've learned from this soul detox. Which strategies will you continue to use, which were the most effective, and what didn't work for you?

NOTES

$\mathcal{D}ay$ 30

Celebrate!!

oday is your day to celebrate. There's no assignment today, just a celebration. The way I usually celebrate is to go to the beach alone. It soothes me, calms me, and allows me to be one with myself. I just walk around with my journal or camera and write about or take pictures of things that make me smile.

If you don't want to do that, then celebrate the way you usually do. I just want you to be happy and proud of your achievement. Tell yourself that you love yourself and what a special person you are. Don't let *anything* make you feel less than who you are and can be.

By the last day, you'll feel like a successful computer hacker. You have just hacked through the most complicated computer system – namely the human brain – and have molded it according to what you wanted. You allowed your brain to get rid of the negative microchips living in it and installed new positive and healthy ones. (My son, who is an engineer, will absolutely be proud of me for this analogy!)

Day 30

NOTES

Postscript

$\mathcal{W}$ell, what a month it has been!! Either you love me right now or you totally hate me for taking you through the roller coaster of emotions that you had to face during this 30 day period.

I want you to understand that neither you nor I have a magic wand that can erase our past and future misfortunes. I truly believe that all of those misfortunes, mishaps or whatever you want to call them are lessons. We're all sent here to learn a few lessons, and once these lessons are learned, we are sent some more. That's why we sometimes stick to our "known" mistakes, because it seems easier to deal with them. We would rather not overcome them because we fear the unknown. What will the next lesson be?

However, the truth is, if we learn strategies to help ourselves overcome our lessons, we will be fully equipped to handle *anything*. Recurring emotions – like anger, fear, jealousy and resentment – will definitely come back, but be aware of them. When you feel anger towards someone, try to understand what triggers you. Is it your ego or the fear of being wrong? Whatever it is, work on the root instead of the anger itself. Find your solitude, sit with yourself, and understand what is happening to you. You were created on this earth to be your own kind, compassionate, crazy, unique self – so just be it! If you do feel depressed, which is something I am very prone to, pull yourself out of it – by yourself.

Don't rely on outward addictions – which can include cigarettes, alcohol, drugs, attention from the wrong people, or even looking for trouble – for relief from your emotional and spiritual pain. Instead, turn to this book. That's why I wrote it. I wanted people to know how to detox their soul. We all know our destination in life, which is basically to love and be loved. But in order to be able to do that, learn how to detox your soul. It's a great path to loving yourself and eventually loving others!